Love & Loss

Epiphanies

Cheryl Lunar Wind
and Friends

Love & Loss

Epiphanies

Any Inquiries contact:

cheryl.hiller@yahoo.com

Some of the poems in this collection first appeared in
We Are One, The Setting Sun and Blessings Beyond Belief
chapbooks, Pleiades and Pensive Journal, Northeastern
University and on facebook.

Cover photo credit to Gary Eagle, 2025

Cover design credit to Catherine Preus, 2025

First edition.

Published by Alexander Agency Books,
Mount Shasta, California 96067

ISBN 979-8-9988971-2-2

Love & Loss

Epiphanies

Preface

In this volume the themes of *Love & Loss* are explored. Messages come from Mount Shasta via mystics and travelers. Over twenty-five fellow humans share their thoughts, feelings and perspective. For those dealing with loss these words can be a soothing balm.

Also, included within are the Universal Laws of Choice and Change, a healing chant for heart activation and a meditation for universal forgiveness.

Love & Loss hints at changes coming and shows that we are the 'heart' of the new earth.

Our Presence is the Sign

We come not as strangers but as something far more prophetic.
More inevitable.
Like the moonlight that lands on our skin.
Like the sunlight untold in the dark.

Our presence is the sign
before the temple doors swing open.

We are the sacred concealed in symbol,
the truth cloaked in myth,
aching for utterance, aching to be spoken.

As thunder knows the contours of the mountain
it was born to stir we are called by name.

---Shane Shema-Sheniy Frojo

Contents

True Happiness
by Valerie Voght

Love precedes Loss making it inevitable.
But when happiness steps in all life feels lighter and brighter.
True happiness comes forward to illumine all life.
Hummingbirds and butterflies twitter with a happy flitting
from plant to plant especially those in full bloom.

Petrified
by Jennifer Hershelman

Dancing Trees, singing in the petrified forest

Decomposition, the witness to changes of life

Loss, the return to beauty

Death, the essence of life   reinvented
reclaimed
returned
renewed
reborn

Lost Love reclaimed

The magic of the forest

Reborn

Tightrope Walker
by Shivrael

Pink Sprinkles walks the edge between worlds.
She carries a basket and a drum.
She throws stardust of remembrance-
for those who can see through the veils, like she does.

She awakens with her presence.
Her land prayers are sung
in forgotten tongues that activate.

Pink Sprinkles holds a mirror
to your distortions
So that our world can heal.
She is a poet,
A presence,
A priestess.

She is someone from between worlds-
A bridge from one reality to the next.

She is meant to be here
in a sacred purpose
that no one understands
But is important.

Love & Loss
by Timothy Hershelman

The game of magic and heartbreak.

Enjoy the butterflies and have some humility,
or end up like a train off it's tracks.

Even trees decompose or become petrified eventually,
so be delicate as you witness life.

Be open to pivot and reinvent yourself,
just ask the butterflies, anything is possible with change.

Lost
by Cheryl

She's hard to let go of---
like an unrequitted love.

"these stones I carried as long as I could,
these stones I loved as long as I could."*

A cold sweat crawling
up my leggs and down my back.

A beginning and end---
there is no in between.

Just an uneasiness of something important
Gone.

What I lost I can't remember,
but I know
it will never be the same.

*George Sefaris

Tears
by Cheryl

Tears
Open our minds---
Crack the shell of our consciousness.

I Am vulnerable---
because I Am free to be me.

My strength comes from my weakness.

My pain makes me beautiful---

An innocent's tears are more powerful
than
a warrior's sword.

Crazy Train
by Cheryl and Catherine

All aboard
Come ride the crazy train.

Scream till your hoarse, can't breathe and gotta pee--
then just collapse.

It's actually good to laugh at life.

So Ozzy--
You saw it coming--
Are you there now?
We are.

Funny thing...
Reading Stephen King's *Lisey's Story*
has actually helped with this transition.

I'm going to *Boo'ya Moon* to sit
and watch the 'Hollyhocks'.

6

Spin Your Tires
by Cheryl

Laugh until you cry.
Then let go of all hope--

Constantly holding on,
becomes too much.
Wants and desires
bring harm.
Judgment
about how 'things should be'

End
in broken glass (shattered dreams)

Re-living painful moments,
Keeps you stuck
Tires spinning, mud flying
not going anywhere--

Do I need a driving lessons?
I thought I had it figured out--
Was doing ok...
Fuck.
I do not. I am not.

Marry Gratitude
by A'Marie B. Thomas-Brown

Gaining lost ground in the silence that's so loud
The screams and moans releasing a buildup tension that seeks
comfort
That seeks understanding
Comprehension even
Amid briars and thistles that conjugate among roses
Suppressing voice frequencies that I observe in unamused delight
For the sake of elevation
I'm facing
The hidden opposition
Amid my choosing to accept the unacceptable
Making peace with the argument abled
Understanding that it's always my ball
Always my court
I choose divorce in the name of Holy Matrimony
Aside from lost dichotomies
That scream
Peace
So I walk down the aisle
Aromatically
Decidedly
Choosing interruption
As a bridge to close the gap
Left gaping with the words
It's all good
Hearing the sound of every silent response
Creating space for me to respond
Or expand
Do you take Gratitude to be your energetic station
To have and to hold
From this exchange forward
As long as you shall live
I do
I now pronounce you here
Walk in the liberty that was created
Long before language attached to a sound
With the power to heal
To deliver
To set free

Every captive
That won't let you be
So breathe
And keep breathing
Until you see
That what you are looking for
You already have
And the shift
Has the power
To mend every rift
Elusively present
In the desert of my own conviction
Beyond trial and jury
Benched judgment
Verdict rendered
A heart tendered
In every I do
That leaves the door open
To further dialogue
Hope's initiation
The wine of evolution
Sipped at the appropriate time
On the hinges of the Eternal plow
I am well endowed
With every breath
In every frenetic frequency
Encountered
In stillness
So subtly
That it breaks the sound barrier
Transmuting love
Upward from the cliff
The precipice
As the movie credits role
My name in lights
Iridescent glow
I'm in the flow
Gotta go
Opened eyes see
It's all good
Breathe

Penned. 2/16/2023
And so we breathe...

Above & Beyond
by Janine Savient

I see you...
I see you beyond the body
I see you above your fear

Our hearts are one...
In purity
LOVE - the reason we're here

We come for the experience
Realization... is our aim
Within every tangible moment,
we play within loves game

Is your heart open...
Is your mind softened down
Are you willing ...
Are you ready...
To play the only game in town

Love...

It's all about love
The joy of it
The coy of it
The light it is
The bite it gives
The play it brings
The song it sings
The connection through...
Both me and you

Loves presence here
Loves absence - fear

Loves deeper knowing
Loves ecstasy glowing

It warms my heart
To know we're a part...
Of loves truest connection
10

Deep bonds of affection

Each other's reflection
Within Loves utter

Perfection
And...
No matter what you find yourself in
Love always, ALWAYS...
Has the win

The Law of Choice
by Naomi Nash

Maiden,
Mother,
Inner Crone
Dance, the vibration of our magical moon.
Pivots change
the Inner-Play

As humming silence
is here to stay.
Indelible beauty,
Reinvents the possible
Sweet composition
of the Soul.

As humility witnesses life
Practicing dying
Without strife!
On bless'ed train tracks
of love's return
Reclaimed Harmony,
Ever burns

Earth;
A science project on Love, Frequency, Vibration
Pure intent from above.
In Joy
We energize the trees,
Soaking in
The singing bees.
Dancing to
our heart's content
In silence too
LOVE's assignment
Laws and choices of abundance
Delicate
Our Sacred chance.

Learning how
to glide like honey
Blazing forth our harmony

Beam the witness
of our journey
Painting truth,
our energies.

Panther Meadows
by Naomi Nash

Come home to dine with mother now
Come home to sit with her awhile
Return home for dinner now
with Mother Earth, we ever vow
Come home and sleep upon your bed
Let angels brush your breath and head

Finding Love (Upper Sand Flat, Mt. Shasta)
by Marya Summers

How long have you spent waiting?
How long have you looked down the dusty road,
hoping to see your beloved emerge from a beautiful wood?

When did you learn to equate love with longing?
        With emptiness?
        With despair?
        With a lonely road?

When did you forget the forest? Forget yourself?

Take your eyes off the road.
Look around all that surrounds you. This is love.

Then close your eyes and come home.
Abide softly in the place where there is no waiting & no road.
Fullness of love that never arrives or leaves.

The Congregation
for my fellow travelers
by Marya Summers

We are each wayfarers, navigating our craft,
finding grace as we steer a course by the stars.
But some hearts truly let go to wild, embodied faith
with apparently little to nothing between themselves & danger,
daring to venture where spirit leads into a giving web that meets
each need.

In Southern Oregon, the same heat that gathers golden plums into
sweetness collects young men in the shadow of a bank.
Fox & Tarzan offer gracious conversation and easy laughter.
Even their stories move like vagabonds, wandering yet purposeful.
From my camper, I bring breakfast.
Our wealth is open hearts, extended hands, bare feet.

On Mount Shasta, grandmothers make homes on wheels,
trusting their vehicles' safe passage as fires swallow forest.
In the smoke & ash of hubris mingle the small clouds of our pipe
ceremony, elevating incineration to a new start. Hummingbird
smears bear fat and red ochre on our foreheads and we shake
rattles under the firs and call in the spirit of healing.

Alone I often do not see my divinity and cannot separate
my circumstances from my worth, but among other chrysalis souls,
I awake to imminence: not just a tragedy of illness & disability
but a miracle of breath and dirt.

We are one body blessed by the struggle of forging faith from
calamity, each ministering to each.
Wherever two or more gather--
a community, a church, a home, a choir.

Moon Magic (For Madeline)
by Anna Scheving

We are decomposing at the same time we are reinventing.
Moonbeams of light become darkness.
It's the inevitable ebb and flow of dancing life and practicing dying.

I am a Witness to Life
by Anna

In death I sing as my sacred breath blows into eternal emptiness.
Into the All is One song of limitless vibrations.

Heartbreak
by Anna

I let go of my mind's heartbreak
to solely feel the fluttering of my internal heartstrings.
They are fragile and weak but already becoming stronger
through my superconscious remembrance of who I really am.

A Poem for Jamian
by Shima Moore, fma Judi V. Brewer, June 9, 1989

I awoke this morning
still entangled in unfinished dreams,
visions of suffering, of terminal illness,
yet joyous, with thoughts of karma terminated

AIDS transformed,
as I sensed all beings, whose suffering
in their last months, years or weeks, was a critical opportunity
A completion of karmic cycles in this, and perhaps many lifetimes,
one's own karma and maybe even that of humanity.

Regeneration and rebirth,
a modern-day crucifixion
Resurrection, the ultimate outcome.

"And the Angels of Light descend to guide us home...celebrating
freed from bondage to soar into the next cycle. Free to merge
into the Light and Love of the Eternal Being who IS the
Beginning and the End."

I smiled as I got it: And at last, your suffering made sense.

Sacred Epiphanies
by Mikasa Tamara Blue Ray

The world you knew,
a weary stage
Turns now a revolutionary page.

The "matrix grid"
a blinding plight.

Implodes and fades out of sight.
Observe the fragments as they fall,
And answer freedom's loud call.

The Plan is Changing
through Dave Harvey

Your planet is capable of support you cannot yet imagine,
for if you could it would appear.

We are telling you this for motivation, not ridicule.
Your plan was to forget.
Your plan was to be here when the plan changes.
The plan is changing.

-The Ancients

Knowing
through Dave Harvey

Some will hold onto beliefs after they no longer make sense,
this applies to the aware as well as the unaware.

Survival instincts are the last to go,
nobody wants to be wrong.

Lighten up and realize you need to know nothing.

-AlTah Rah

Reclamation
by Cheryl

So much gratitude
for the silent trees--
even with heartbreaks,
train wrecks and love & loss.

I am reclaimed, reinvented--

I can dance with change,
pivot like a ballerina.

At times---I'm petrified--

Be a witness to Life's abundance.

Feel the vibration of music,
singing, humming, drumming.

Dance In Joy
like Butterflies do.

Claim Your Inner Beauty & Humility.

All things are possible--
It is the indelible truth.

*Return to the Love you Lost.
Witness your own Reclamation.

Message from the Butterflies
by Shivrael

Returning to ashes
Returning to dust
is what our body does
at the end of an incarnation.

Yet the spirit we are
returns to the soul place
where we infinitely exist
in the non-physical,
united in oneness with soul family,
as beings of light, playing.

Earth is not for the weak.
Why do we come back again, anyway?
Why, it's for the experience
that our souls long for-
Or maybe it is the singing and dancing?

Bliss is possible.
Let's find it.
No more practicing dying.
Let's find what makes our hearts sing
before we go back to the soul place
as we allow our mortal bodies to decompose
returning to the Earth again..

We are here for a moment
as the butterflies are.
Let's remember to
smell the flowers
as they do.

Flutters and Pirouettes
by Elizabeth Carrillo

A delicate harmony in the silence
of the playfulness amongst the trees.

An indelible abundance in the musical
harmony amongst the bees.

The beauteousness of sparkly pink butterflies
of lemony yellow and orangy orange ones, too
join the super drums of the pine cones
pivoting in joy to fall towards... YOU!

And you... A witness to Life!!! Phew!!!
Whoa!!! (Inhale and breathe it all in)

Eating manna while you sing and dance
and hoot and holler
...and pause
...and wonder
and breathe in again.

And speak of your heartbreaks
and pivots in life...

inevitable, indelible, possible
decomposition of your life:

That delicate stage only seen
by the diminutive lady bug
who felt your hot tears fall
so heavy on her ruby bodice...

Yet she remained.
steady, steady, oh so steady still
on the bracelet you reinvented
and reclaimed as
your magical amulet of self-love.

Ohhh yeah... I'm magical
Ohhh YEAH!
Truth!

The same energy that creates
Moon Magic;
that allows us to practice
dying each second
with each choice we make!

Same frequency... A new me, you, we!

It's the same magic and vibration to reclaim, remember, and BE!

Note to Self:
That change is a pivot
and that pivot is a pirouette!

Fittingly, that magical darling of a ladybug
flutters and pirouettes away
leaving inner joy and knowing
in her wake.

HA OH (Healing Activation Open Heart)
chant by Hope

Ma Ga Ba La Da Ra
Nu Ki So Ti Zo We

Sha Hu Va Na Za La
Ki Mo Du Je Wu He

Line 1: Heal and activate the body
Line 2: Heal and activate the mind
Line 3: Heal and activate the spirit
Line 4: Combine together to open the heart

Ma Ga Ba La Da Ra
*Heal and activate the body

Nu Ki So Ti Zo We
*Heal and activate the mind

Sha Hu Va Na Za La
*Heal and activate the spirit

Ki Mo Du Je Wu He
*Combine together to open the heart

Syllable Meanings:

Line 1: Ma Ga Ba La Da Ra – Body Activation

Ma – Earth, mother, origin (body grounding)
Ga – Earth, nourishment, generation
Ba – Breath, soul, foundation
La – Light, rhythm, harmony
Da – Giving, foundation
Ra – Sun, life force, activation

Activate the body with earth energy, breath, and solar vitality.

24

Line 2: Nu Ki So Ti Zo We – Mind Activation

Nu – Name, vibration, essence
Ki – Spirit, blueprint, cosmic structure
So – Truth, purity, cosmic law
Ti – Earth, stability, manifestation
Zo – Beginning, essence, energy
We – Unity, wholeness, harmony

*Awaken the mind with truth, clarity, and unified awareness.

Line 3: Sha Hu Va Na Za La – Spirit Activation

Sha – Divine presence, purification
Hu – Breath, spirit, divine will
Va – Wind, motion, breath of life
Na – Essence, vibration, name
Za – Origin, primal energy
La – Light, harmony, rhythm

Elevate the spirit with divine breath, motion, and sacred origin.

Line 4: Ki Mo Du Je Wu He – Heart Opening

Ki – Spirit, blueprint, cosmic structure
Mo – Mother, memory, cosmic rhythm
Du – Give, sustain, cosmic law
Je – Illumination, calling, divine presence
Wu – Unity, nothingness, source
He – Breath, spirit, divine presence

Mud Magic
by Cheryl

Who you gonna call?
The Dirty Girls--
We are the mudslingers at our best.

We are heroines
skilled in the ways
of mud magic.

They say food is medicine--
I say mud is medicine.

Rub it all over your body & dance a jig.

Give thanks to the
Divine Mother
who loves us dearly.

Don't worry about getting dirty--
It'll all come out in the wash.

Mud Dancer
by Jennifer Hershelman

Mud mania
Mud palooza
Mud mastery
Mud crafters
Mud whispers
Mud slingers

Mud cakes
Mud creatures

Mud bear
Mud worlds
Mud love

Out

Love & Loss
by Shima Moore

Witnessing life and the Moon's magic
through eyes of mother, maiden, crone
reclaimed & reinvented
We rise.

Petrified in humility
and indelible heartbreak,
our inevitable decomposition

Butterflies, trees, love & loss
The return of beauty
And music's delicate inner play

Dipped in honey
In its energy, frequency and vibration
soaring in joy
dancing and singing harmony

Until we pivot, with change
practice dying
eternally silent

Ponders
by Maggie Barto

Walking along the train track,
will a train come by?
Wait, the tracks are rusty
no trains today.

What's prettier, a butterfly or a dragonfly?
Mabe a dragonfly--I like them better.
Don't know why. I just do.

Is everything a possibility? Not Sure.
I live on a beautiful mountain,
but I will never climb.
I live near a beautiful river,
but I will never fish.
It's ok--Others will.

I have lavender bushes,
bees come to gather the pollen.
Wish I could taste the honey.
I do love the sound of buzzing,
that's enough.

Lots of inner thoughts--all the time.
Are they meaningful thoughts? maybe

When the magic moon is full
my room is lit with beautiful light.
Don't go away moon, I feel your warmth.
Sadly, the moon left,
and now it's dark.

Day Out of Time: Meditation for Universal Forgiveness
source unknown

Begin by finding a quiet, comfortable place. Focus on your breath.

Let your body settle into stillness. You might place your hands over your heart.

Now, speak (silently or aloud):

I offer forgiveness to all I have harmed (knowingly or unknowingly).

I offer forgiveness to all who have harmed me (knowingly or unknowingly).

I forgive myself for the ways I have abandoned, betrayed, or dimmed my own light.

I forgive the forgetting.

I release the need to understand.

I release the need to punish.

I release the looping narratives that keep pain alive.

I choose coherence.

I choose healing.

I choose remembrance.

I choose love.

Remain in silence, allowing these words to resonate deeply within your heart.

Feel the release move through your body, and then extend into the earth, into the places that still hold war, pain, and fragmentation.

Offer your compassion to all beings.
Let your light ripple outward.
Release what is no longer yours to carry.

Yellow Seed Day: A New Galactic Year
by Vivian McIntosh

Going back to the Ancient Age of The Mayan
A Day Out Of Time, the season of Leo the Lion

Embrace the essence of super charged energy
Powerful portals opened to illuminate our memory

Help out humanity by celebrating Galactic Freedom Day with me-
July 25 is also my born day! Woo-hoo, Yippee!!!

The day after New Year's Eve, but before New Year's Day
Sounds magically mysterious and kinda curious to say

It's simple for us to step up and into Timelessness
Only costs you a quick change of consciousness

Start by seeing the world in ALL its True Beauty
Realize it's everyone entangled in a Divine Unity

Never been us vs them, that's playing into the programmed
problem--Think and speak different than you did before, make a
leap of quantum

Take a truthful look inside of your temple to detox your heart, mind
and gut--Treasures were placed inside our DNA, just like in the
tomb of King Tut

Face yourself, in others you'll find a mirror,
reflect on choices over the past year
Own every lesson, embrace victories,
then you'll create integrity that's crystal clear

Let go of the past and calmly wave goodbye to the end of a cycle
Ring in a Bright New Year and Beginning, develop into a Christlike
disciple

Open your heart and mind, dont miss out on this opportunity of an
Opening Act--
The Lion's Gate Portal is bringing in an abundance of potential, and
that's a fact

The yellow couch
by Dmitriy Butler

I'm sitting on a yellow couch in an alley between houses ,
I'm distant at the same distance from all the oceans
I'm in the center and at the same time out of time , out of space -
I'm on a yellow sofa , it's like a ship for me to fly into space ,
where there is nothing but you , except for your heart
Everyone has this place, outside of space and time,
but not everyone is able to trust it enough to dissolve and become
just that place,
an extension or bridge from the reality where you are someone
and the place where you are not, but you know that you exist,
even though there is no proof.
Talking to yourself, talking to God...
That's what my soul was waiting for, sitting on that yellow couch
with me.

Short Ones
by Tim and Cheryl

Sun warming my skin.
The glare blinding both my eyes.
Summer's love rolls on. **--Tim**

Wind piercing through me.
Twist throttle under my grip.
The Solice for me. **--Tim**

Blowing Wind by Cheryl

I am White Wind
and the wind is blowing....

I do not need AI to help me write.
We are above and beyond such things.

Remember...
the Divine Plan.

Now is the time
to create a new way....

You can follow or lead,
doesn't matter to me...
Just come along.

Mt. Shasta Kigo by Cheryl

cold crows
snowflakes,
bring seclusion
the mountain sleeps under
her white blanket.

Illumination from the Inside
by Shivrael

Welcome elementals
(The tiny ones)
Welcome fae-
share the magic of your light
How do you turn on
your inner illumination?

We are releasing as we become
the stars that we are.
We know that we are
beyond human,
beyond Earth.
We are from everywhere
and everywhen.

Some of us came from the future.
To shift this realm
so that all embody
light and love
including our beloved Mother Earth.
Let us shine
as stars.

We remember our divinity.

Soul of Truth
by Mikasa Tamara Blue Ray

Heaven on Earth;
Sacred Mother Arc Anchored!
When a Soul of Truth does shine.
Reflecting light, a pure design.
The hollow forms, cannot stay.
They turn and flee, run away.

Observe the world, a stage so wide.
Where many wear a mask to hide.

A polished smile, a practiced gaze.
Through life they wander, lost in haze.

But when a Soul of Truth does shine.
Reflecting light, a pure design.

The hollow forms, cannot stay.
They turn and flee, run away.

For authenticity, a beacon bright.
Exposes shadows to the light.

The masks they wear begin to fray.
Revealing truths they can't quite sway.

So mind not, souls of depth and grace.
When empty smiles vacate their space.

Your inner compass, firm and true.
Points to the paths meant just for you.

Receive peace, know your worth.
Be the truest ground upon this earth.

Let pretense vanish from your sight.
And walk steadfastly in your light.

Let It Be
by Rune Darling

You Are
The Alpha
The Omega
The First
The Last
The Beginning
The End
.

Soon The World Falls Into Place
Be The Voice of Reason
You Will Do It Well
.

Face Your Own Demons
Let Them Guide You Through The Maze
.

Like Ask And Embla (Adam and Eve)
Together We Will Fly
Its Just You And Me
Mother Mary - Let It Be
.

From All Four Chambers Of Our Heart
We Are Humans After All

The Tree of Life And Love Is About
To Make the Blue Sirius Star Come Out
.

Children of The Sun
Take Care of The Earth
.

The Titans Return
The Dimension Of Five Shall Birth
.

The BlueBirds Shall Break The Cage
Love Unleashing Now In Hera's Age
.

In You All Things Hold Together
Now You See What Is Meant To Be
.

How Life On Earth Can Be
Your Soul Wants It - Now You See
Your White Hearts Open - Let It Be

.

In The Power Of Now
There's No Point In Placing Blame
You Should Know We Suffer The Same

.

Let's All Melt Our Hearts
And Never Be Apart

.

Give Yourself To Me
We All Hold A Key

.

Hold On
With Love
Rune Darling

____Bedknobs and Broomsticks____
by Cheryl

What are bedknobs for anyway?

Are they like doorknobs,
turning them before sleep--
to set a location?

Lefty loosey
Righty tighty

Sleep being the doorsill---

Is it like in 'Howl's Moving Castle'
Setting a gage---
before opening the door?

<------------------->
 Law of Choice

Left or Right?
Which way to go?
You decide.

Sphere Of Conscious Dreams
by Rune Darling

Has Been Created
Has Been Activated
.

The Key Turned Again
Unlocking Next Phase
.

The World A Stage For Miracles
The Clay Formed By Our Own Hands
.

We The Creators Shall Mold
Stardust Into Fabric Of Earthly Life
.

Now The Collective Will Dream Plasma
The Foundation Of Remembering
.

Rapidly Deteriorating The Veil
Acceleration Of Awakening
.

My Will Molds The Future
Maybe Yours Too
.

Hello Again
by Shivrael

Meet you in the depths
of soul recognition.
We'll peel away the layers
of one another.
We will go so deep
to the place our soul recalls
Who we are.
All the stories of Atlantis
and Lemuria.
Cosmic recollection
Collated in memory of the Akashic Records.

Why do you bring up such
from my depths?

Soul's Recognition
by Pradeep Nawarathna

you look at me like you've never seen eyes so deep
and somehow you seep into my soul
like you were meant to be there

i'm falling
as you come closer
and there's nowhere else i want to be

you speak to my heart
in a language it understands
touching every insecurity with such tenderness

this happened so fast
this meeting of souls
yet it feels like you were always mine

now i can't imagine
a single moment without you
maybe this is what love is supposed to do

Daisies
by Maya Rawitch

They set down their guns, in the wet yellow grass,
and look their captor in the eye and hold them there.

They set down their words,
shove them back into the dark mouth crevice,
once they realize the wounds they have inflicted.

He takes the next train home to the little girls and boys sat quietly
gathered round the clock cause daddy will be home soon.

She sets down her pen,
tired of slaving away for letters and steps outside,
so she can let the lonely sun soak into the gap that lay empty of
warmth inside her.

We crumple our mistakes, chew on them like the vitamin d3
lozenge that staves off a july depressive episode,
stomp on the ink until the red ink splotches run off to Gaza like the
dead sea parting, and life will go on.

I pick a daisy in a blossoming gossamer field
and let the grass envelop me until time runs still.

We gather together with joint synovial fluid saturated arms
and collective genuine smiles.
Faded grief and parted dead seas swirling in our eyes.
The dead don't gather, the dead don't speak, let alone see.
But what you can't see, can't scare you.

And yet...
as WE part, WE remember.

The White Subaru
by Maya Rawitch

She sits in my white Subaru,
balls of her feet digging into the mat
meant to protect her from the heat.
She lets her gaze drift out the window,
trying to will the pine tree's sappy scent
to sift into her nostrils so she can ground
back down to planet Earth.

She steps out of the car,
her bare feet a stark contrast
to the black pavement.
She runs alongside the car as if
the road had turned into a race track
and the empty houses cheering neighbors.
She stops at the stop sign like a good law abiding citizen
and stands there,
silently repeating the numbers on the license plate
until the car becomes not but a speck of matter,
passively diffusing ever so slowly towards the horizon.

Possible
by Kylie Makinson

The train tracks stretch out before me in a sallow yawn.
I practice my death on these tracks,
gently pawing my flip flop along the rail before plopping
down across them to my imaginary demise.
I lay in wait for my doom,
spread out like a movie heroine that no one is coming for.

Instantly, it is night.
Butterflies dance, the moon is high,
and chimney smoke fills the air with silence.

Do they know I'm dying?

The trees are shrouded in black as they answer me in riddles,
the stars twirl above me in circular lines like a swirling drain--

As I close my eyes to what is possible

Keep On
by Pradeep Nawarathna

I want you to know— you are incredible.
You've walked through storms you never called for,
carried burdens no one should bear.
You were talked down to,
bruised by words and moments that never saw your worth.
And still— you kept going.
You stood when you could've curled up.
Smiled when you wanted to disappear.
Breathed through pain so heavy it nearly stole your voice.

You never quit. And that matters.
Even now, if you're still in the middle of it, still aching,
still reaching...You're still here.
You're still rising.
And one day, you will look back—
and whisper to yourself, "I made it."
Even though once you thought you wouldn't.
Be proud of that. Be proud of you.
There's an extraordinary life ahead,
woven just for your kind of courage.
So don't stop now.
Even when the path is steep, even when the light grows dim—
Keep walking.
And if you can't feel proud of yourself yet, let me remind you:
I am. I see you. I honor you.
Always.

Our Presence is the Sign
by Shane Shema-Sheniy Frojo

We come not as strangers but as something far more prophetic.
More inevitable.
Like the moonlight that lands on our skin.
Like the sunlight untold in the dark.

Our presence is the sign
before the temple doors swing open.

We are the sacred concealed in symbol,
the truth cloaked in myth,
aching for utterance, aching to be spoken.

As thunder knows the contours of the mountain
it was born to stir we are called by name.

Recovery
by A'Marie B. Thomas-Brown

I swab myself
To feed my denied addiction
Until the wall falls
As the monitor registers a faint heartbeat
The place where hope is realized or dies
In this fabled state
I garner a hope
That others can use the information
To define me on their own terms
I recover as a recluse
In this imaginary place
That deceptively provides me
The strength that I need
To further exist in this way
With the words continually silenced
Enabling me
To concoct a story
In the hopes
That someone will believe me

Healing
by Bodhi Holum Johnson

Some think it's all a game
The biggest part of recovery
Is the guilt and the shame
The remnants of pain
The anxiety that comes now and again
There's worth in the work
It's within your control
Discipline the mind
Sends silence to the noise
It's a truth that many share
A walk in love to be self aware
To listen to everything you hear
To feel as though you're seeing here
Seeing through the darkness of ourselves
These are honest truths we face
To bring about heaven or hell
Once you have made it this far
There is no turning back
Just you in the beauty that you are
Above the chaos
That turns wounds into scars

Feel your soul
by Bodhi Holum Johnson

I wear the scars of yesterday
Even though it's all an illusion
Delusions of contusions
That reveal the rips to every scar
Every nik that was my fault
Every rip burns its painful face
Sends messages of the world we create
That we've been unconscious for too long
That we need to unite and be strong
Let us live together
Better weather in our neter
Within to without
Over any dollars of doubt
Let the money go
Sit down with yourself and feel your soul
That's me in there too
Every thing you say and do
Is constructs of what you creating through
The vibrations of your being
Body mind and spirit
Silence your mind and you'll hear it
Flowers of seeds
That keep moving energy
Constant is your state of being
Be here be clear
Feel free to be
It's simple grooves in simplicity
Everything is happening
For reasons we've been hearing
Through the Ages the years of awakening

Heart Games
by Cheryl

Love & Loss
Up & down
Here we go
For another Round--

Round and Round
We go
Where we stop
No body knows

the long and winding road
to my heart

Bring it
by Shivrael

Drop into clarity.
Drop a pebble into the well
of infinity
hear it reach the bottom
as ripples rise.
You are those ripples
bringing a new frequency
to the collective.

From the clarity;
The peace that you feel within
arises the change
that you wish to see
in the world.

You are that change.

To the pebble droppers,
rabble rousers
game changers
This is for you.
We celebrate your uniqueness!

Better Days
by Maya Rawitch

Love & Loss reciprocate,
bounce off of one another and tap, tap, tap
at the edge of my conscious awareness like a renegade relapsing,
collapsing--
obsessively holding on to the thought of better days ahead.

I practice dying as I lay in my desk casket,
feel like I'm stripped of my ego, lying at the end of a train track
watching and waiting for delirium to shut my eyes
and terror to push forth a scream from my parched & withered lips.

As I witness the caboose nearing my left ear,
I hear the solemn whisper of abundance grace my chest.
I let it ride to fill both hemispheres of my tired out lonely brain.

The return of beauty to my sullen cheeks is much celebrated by the
butterflies that land atop my nose.

I am petrified in humility as a bee rushes past me, the grandest
creator of honey that has ever lived has just skimmed my eyelashes
and graced me with its presence.

Inner play has me in disarray, I have forgotten the so-called wisdom
of my 9-5 corporate decomposing flesh body that demands I pluck
every piece of wisdom inevitable, indeliable--
Pluck them off the great big tree of my mind like gooseberries--
not to be confused with poison berries.

Brevity need not be confused with clarity.
Levity levitates its grey fog over me.

Moon magic.
Witch hatchet.

Love casts a glow on the moon shadow.
I need not run for it, catch up to it---
It's right here inside my body,
it harbors peace & comfort willingly.
It caresses me in its safety.

The corporate shadow has got to be slain.

I will slay this beast through dancing, musical inquiry,
singing, drumming, humming,
becoming energy, frequency and vibration.

Reclaimed
Reinvented
Restored
Relived
Remorse

Come forth into the silence and praise the Good Lord
that you are free at long last!

The Age Of Eyes
by Kazi Ayaz Mahesar

The Age of Eyes
Is as old as Universe

Perhaps Eyes
Are more ancient

When even skies
Did not exist

When even the Creator
Had no plans to create

Yes Eyes
Were the first to see

To see and wonder
At such an emptiness

To see and think
What to make of it

The stars came as a thought
And angels its manifestation

And the Age-less
Thought of the age

Of a beginning
And an end

And smiled
At its own thought

Like a child
And its play

The Sea
And a sandcastle

The World
To become a wave

A Trough
And a Crest

A boat
And a sail

All in the Eyes
To break

All in the Eyes
To make.

.

Rebirth
by Shivrael

Will the monkey mind ever become quiet?

Ram Ram Ram polishes
the mirror of the soul
so it is clean.
Hanuman serves from
a place of love.

In meditation and in life
you are invited to
surrender into the arms of divine.
You are held and supported
always in all ways.

Just let go-
this is the key
which turns the sanctity
of your pure heart-
illuminating all beings.

I rest in the amrita,
the sweetness of divine,
flowing in 108,000 nadis.

I AM more that this body.
I remember
our true identity
which is oneness.

When this body ends
they will burn it
as they do in India.

We remember this:
We exist eternally.

After all life's experiences
and remembrances,
I AM all this and more-

beyond past lives, incarnations
that all lead to this precious moment
so let us savor it's sweetness fully.

You are given superpowers
when you choose
to be in service forever.

Even in the same life
you can be born again.

Reborn
by Jennifer Hershelman

Keep dancing Pink Sprinkles
to find your heart centered path,
you must allow yourself
to be humbled by your own
inner truth, with impeccable honesty.

Journey Inward
become intimate with your shadows.
Dance with Buttercups
in fields of yellow flowers,
and learn healthy boundaries.

Let the joyful energy
of singing your freedom
banish your doubts and cast
powerful protection
on your new paths
of unconditional love.

God Within
by Rune Darling

AIR CONTROL TO DARLING
.

This Is The Final
CountDown To Consciousness
CountDown New Earth
Evolution
.

Lift Off To Love
.

I AM
YOU ARE
WE ARE
.

ONE for All
And All For One
.

God Within -- Will Hear You
God Within -- Will Hear You
God Within -- Will Hear You

I Am: We Are
by Cheryl

When you step into your I Am--
you become the great We Are.

It is the great return.
Who else feels it?

It is glorious to live
connected and free---
like the plants and animals,
just doing their thing
not worrying; all in harmony,
naturally,
Not--
Underdressed, Overdressed
Open, Closed----Fitting in?
Wondering...
Do I belong--
SQueezing ourselves into boxes---
Shrinking down so as to please---

Wanting to be a part,
of something, anything--
Not realizing
We Are the Great I Am.

We Stand Out. No longer
able to hide.
We are tall. Towering. Like Tor.*
This is our tower moment.

We will not go quietly. Not silenced--
any more.

We Are.

*Glastonbury Tor

Love Poem for the Abandoned Child
by Marya Summers

For too long, child, you
have chased the hearts
of those who deserted their own
surveying pinched faces
parched terrain
for family for a place
to call home, still
looking to prove your worth
in the conversion
of the loveless

Soon, you will begin to quietly build
Yourself a home within yourself
Around the hearth that was always there

Love will blossom as you gather years
Like wildflowers, as you look at a meadow
Like a mirror, seeing your own wild

Beauty on the weathered face of a mountain
You will reach back into your history
Invoking the love of generation, of generations

You will feel in your heart the calm
Beating of lifetimes of unstruck power and
Become a thundercloud releasing the blessed rain

Child by Cheryl

Grandmothers are there for you
when
mothers are busy--
with the business of living,

working, taking care of the younger children,
cooking dinner, partying, playing bingo and
other important things.

When I was in the hospital
recovering from a suicide attempt---

It was my grandnother
that came to see me.

Poor mom--
she really didn't have a clue.

My mother---
often so busy
keeping busy--
that life passed by.

She was not there when I needed her---
there is an empty,
painful place
that will not be filled.

It's sad when parents
don't give their children
the love and support,
they need
But,
We can.
Love ourselves--
the inner child
who feels sad--

Give her
the support, attention and love
that she deserves.
61

Listen
by Cheryl

Dorothy takes flight--

Alice tumbles--

Whole worlds exist
in the strangest places--
on a dandelion bloom.

If you listen carefully,
you will hear them.

The Walrus recites poetry,
and a rabbit keeps time.

Plants are always watching--
they witness--
our ups and downs,
our dramas.

You can talk to them--
If they like you
they will talk back.

Listen.
Be like Horton,
Who do you hear?

Who are we?
by Cheryl

I used to think that we were like
Horton (Horton Hears a Who)
listening for small voices from the many
universes we live among.....in the natural
world on Mother Earth--the flowers, the trees,
insects, animals and the many unseen beings
who also share this space with us.

I now know we are the small beings,
residing on the dandelion head---
completely engrossed in our day to day lives--
until the wind blows, and we take flight,
scattered all over the surface of planet Earth---
which is nothing but another ball, a sphere--
small in the scheme of things--

Yet interconnected--
like the Music of the Spheres,
our note, tune, vibration--an important addition
to the divine symphony.

We each carry a note adding to the song--
That is why we were seeded here on Earth.
We are the seeds of new Earth.
My seed has a melancholy feel---
a knowing, a wisdom stamped by hardship.

Glimpses of the bigger picture are like commercials in my life.
Can I go there, to that story---
leaving behind the worries and pain
of this little life?
I think so, I have to.
Let it be done.

She Showed Me Who I AM
by Shivrael

On Mount Shasta,
I learned about frequency and vibration.
On Mount Shasta
I lifted my consciousness.
I opened my creativity-
A flood of downloads landed
wanting human expression
and I was there to catch them.

On Mount Shasta
I found drumming.
I danced under the full moon.
I found my inner tribal woman
who is now becoming a crone.
She knows freedom,
She lives in flow,
in a state of expansive delight.
She is an infinite being
of love and light,
as you are, as well.

My heart has opened to myself
with inner acceptance and self-love
how sweet it is!
(I wish you could taste it.)
This is the gift of the mountain.

Curiosity
by Sabina and Herd of Light

Pure curiosity
as a felt sense of openness.
Allow curiosity
to open the senses of the heart
and to ignite the perceptivity
of your whole Being.
Allow curiosity to open
the flood gates of love,
letting love flood in to satisfy
what can not ever be satisfied
by mental constructs.
- with Love,
the Herd of Light

All Will Be Shown
by Le'Vell Zimmerman

God does not need "salesmen" here beloved...
Just like The Sun, it's only necessary for you to shine.

Your greatest service within this hologram is
in the example you set as a reflection for all.
Not the information you share.

All will be shown what they need to see when they need to see it.
Isn't this how awakening happened for you?

This is a sacred process that naturally unfolds
based on your capacity of openness as a Soul.

The Ego Mind identity will continue to remain closed to life itself
in feeling the deceptive intentions of others is a threat,
where your protection is our job as your "Angelic Guardians".

Love is open and fearless(expanding).
Fear is closed and defensive(contracting).

It's a free will choice beyond the judgments of right or wrong
amongst others what you choose to entertain/ cultivate.

This has always been about trusting yourself and how it feels...

You are always "unconditionally supported".

-The Angels

Until
by Kazi Ayaz Mahesar

Until
No one is elder to me
Until
No one is younger
Until
I am of all ages
And of all times
Until
I am all the lands
And all the skies
Until
I am ancient
Than all the ancients
Until
I am ancestor
Of all the ancestors
Until
I am all the beginning
Until
I am all the infinity
Until then
I am Here
To become
THAT!

When you know who you are
by Tahlia Hunter

When you know who you are
Other people can enter and exit your life
Without it rocking your world
As your foundation is solid and unshakable
Because you have yourself.

When you know who you are
The opinions and judgments of others matter far less
And people can speak words of criticism,
unkindness and malice about you
Without it affecting how you feel about yourself.

When you know who you are
Other people can reject you or abandon you
Without it changing your identity
Because you know that your destiny is not tied
to those who have chosen to leave you
And you feel whole and complete from within.

When you know who you are
You appreciate
That putting your happiness and sense of self-worth
In the hands of another person
Is akin to making them your jailer
And remaining locked in a prison
That only they have the key to rescue you from
While liberating yourself
Means taking full responsibility
For your emotions, identity and well being
And setting yourself free
To live and feel however you may choose.

And when you know who you are
Rather than devoting so much time and energy--
trying to impress others
Or projecting the fulfillment of your own
unmet needs and desires onto them--
You choose to prioritize your own needs and well being,
And make time for your most important relationship
Which is with yourself.

If it ends let it be
by Bodhi Holum Johnson

Merely fragments of smidgbits
I tickle the dragon's paw
I laugh at the face of fear as we all spin around
These intentions are vividly clear
So fast no computing goes near
For everything is here
Be consumed by the conditions that you create
Un condition those and change your fate
There is no grand apocalypse in sight
Just new beginnings and wrongs made right
It's a great time to be you
In all your essence of truth
Let go of the facades
Let them drop like a stone
Watch everyone scatter like drones
Highly programmed to not be comfortable
Just bots in war not seen before
I remain in awe to this day
No matter what may come about
No matter my mistakes
I've entered in my own vibe
I reciprocate or say goodbye
Ta ta goes the same
Change the way you see things
And everything will change
Furthermore iam just as that
No more second guessing
Or doubting my facts
If it ends let it be
Bye an acre or three
Enlighten your body
Detox and be free
Free from the pain and suffering that comes subliminal in your
brains
Free from the trauma that once kept you a slave
Give me breath and I will give it life
In the ways that I create and write
I've come this far to not just come this far
Even if it's here
Or on another star

Letter to My Dead Father
by Maya Rawitch

She is not the girl with wild wind blown hair and rosy cheeks
I knew so well at 12 years of age.
She's battered and broken now, her Nani's a sage.
Tattered and shaken,
wears well worn clothes
and has deep belly aches now.

And yet, there she was...
Performing at the infamous dance recital that I couldn't attend
in 2014 because your mother was trying to take you away from me
because I posed an immediate risk to her children and her safety.
You frolick across the stage,
With a psyche not yet tainted with fear.
She was not yet sworn in to the sorority of sorrow.
She has gained a foot or two, still never cuts her hair,
lets it droop down to her belly button like my face
when I suffered from Bells Palsy...
now foot size is 9 and a half, Big Foot watches her from his perch
in the tunnels of Lumeria etched in the slopes of Mount Shasta.
She stands tall amidst the frenzy,
Don't tell her that she has scoliosis,
her poor posture up ends the muscles in her neck, let it go,
it's not time for her to wake from her slumber.

She surprises me by naming the most obscure of the amino acids
and questioning how adenosine triphosphate undergoes energy
transfer and how entropy transmits light waves into heat energy,
she knows quantum physics, adenosine diposhate be damned.
Still won't look into being a physicist.

Quantum theory is interesting, but the uncertainty is petrifying.
The gut brain axis holds potential,
but are we just scowering for any signs of meaning,
taking and taking when maybe there isn't any for the making?

Light waves, tuning forks, and planets spinning in an untethered
universe are best suited for those lost souls not sutered with
existential dread or avoidant tendencies.

She wants to be a metabolic psychiatrist before she has any babies.
Jewish doctor grandfather is proud, she is carrying on the lineage of sentimentalities.
Her mentality is that of a kosher stoicist, she loves assisting others.
Jesus died at the cross you know.
Why are we worshiping cyclical maladaptive coping strategies?
Jesus is no influence to me, the Buddha is the idol I seek.

This is my voice, not my fathers.
I am not my fathers son, I'm his daughter.
Now, he is of no influence to me.
He will have to leave the job of telling me that I cannot be Jesus to my mother. Jesus is no idol, he died at the cross, and I'm no martyr.

I was his baby girl, now he's up an left me with my beautiful exhausted mother.

Cowboy hats and hearts no longer litter my messages,
you can't leave me on read for two months again
or text me two hundred carefully thought out sentences,
explanations for why you've disappeared,
you're working with horses,
driving away nuisances to Colorado Springs,
tending to your run down Expedition.
I wanted to book a backpacking trip with you through Expedia.

I'm glad my last text to you was I love you and I miss you endlessly.
I still love you effortlessly. You will always be in my heart and your presence will forever take up space in my dreams, you complete me and live within me.
We are both atoms forming a perfect octet and the love is the energy released when the cycle of suffering is upended from a version of nothingness and empty emotional captivity to great emotional proclivity.

I will never let them tarnish the version of you
I carry around in my head, end to end,
I'll travel to the depths of the Earth for you.
If it's a falsity, so be it,
I'd rather be left with a sweet taste in my mouth than risk missing my father's essence and leaving his rough and calloused smile to lay to rest forever at his alter, put on bed rest, ascension is the best bet.

Many thanks to these contributors:

Maggie Barto
A'Marie B. Thomas-Brown
Dmitriy Butler
Elizabeth Carillo
Rune Darling
Shane Shema-Sheniy Frojo
Dave Harvey
Jennifer Hershelman
Timothy Hershelman
Hope
Tahlia Hunter
Bodhi Holum Johnson
Kazi Ayaz Mahesar
Kylie Makinson
Vivian McIntosh
Shima Moore
Naomi Nash
Catherine Preus
Pradeep Nawarathna (pcnawarathna@gmail.com)
Maya Rawitch
Mikasa Tamara Blue Ray
Sabina and Herd of Light
Janine Savient
Anna Scheving
Shivrael
Marya Summers
Valerie Voght
Le'Vell Zimmerman

Author page--

Cheryl Lunar Wind lives in the Mount Shasta area in a little town called Weed. She is a practicer of Mayan cosmology, Lakota ceremony, Star Knowledge and the Universal Laws including the Law of One. Her hobbies are writing poetry, music, dance, drum circles and love for all life; plant, animal and crystal. Cheryl has been a guide and spiritual teacher for many years. Now she shares wit and wisdom through poetry, and has published poetry books; Know Your Way, We Are One, Follow the White Rabbit, Love Your Light, LIFE: Shared thru Poetry, Come to Mount Shasta: Sacred Path Poetry, We Are Light, Finding Our Way Home, We Are Forever, Handshake With the Divine, Grand Rising: A New Day Has Dawned, Star Messages: Codes to Sing, Dance and Live by, Return to Innocence, Bloom Like Nature: Live the Natural Way, Creativity Brings Peace: Create & Share Your Gifts, May Love Lead, The Eventful Flash: Bringing Solar Waves of Change, The Setting Sun, Crossroads of Change, Step Into New Earth, Blessings Beyond Belief-- I Am: We Are, I Love Life and Life Loves Me and now Love & Loss: Epiphanies.

Testimonials---

"Cheryl's poetry is very inspiring--particularly the way she compares life with the forces of nature. There is a special element in her poems that opens my heart and fills my soul with divine possiblities."
Giovanna Taormina, Co-Founder, One Circle Foundation

"Cheryl's poems have helped me to uncover and honor my own hidden memories. The beauty of her spirit is evident in each tender, insightful passage."
Marguerite Lorimer, www.earthalive.com

"A rare collection filled with raw, courageous honesty. Thought provoking words that will stop you in your tracks."
Snow Thorner, ED Open Sky Gallery, Montague, California

"When wisdom, guidance, confirming comfort, ect. arrives to us humans--from beings with the perspective of other realms--it is a divine gift. Especially in the form of what we call poetry, and through a being with no agenda; Cheryl Lunar Wind simply shares what source gives her!"---Dragon Love (Thomas) Budde

www.ingramcontent.com/pod-product-compliance
Lightning Source LLC
Chambersburg PA
CBHW070552030426
42337CB00016B/2457